THE GREEK MUSEUMS

Byzantine Museum

Translation: Brian de Jongh

THE GREEK MUSEUMS

Byzantine Museum

MANOLIS CHATZIDAKIS

Director of the Byzantine Museum

EKDOTIKE ATHENON S.A.

Athens 1994

ISBN 960-213-002-4

PRINTED AND BOUND IN GREECE
by
EKDOTIKE HELLADOS S.A.
An affiliated company
8, Philadelphias Street, Athens

EARLY CHRISTIAN, BYZANTINE AND POST-BYZANTINE ART

BYZANTINE ART

The Byzantine Museum is a unique one in so far as it is exclusively devoted to Byzantine art. To the visitor it may consequently prove to be an extremely useful introduction to the art of this great period in the history of Hellenism. It would not be inappropriate therefore to precede this study with a few essential informative observations regarding the basic characteristics of Byzantine art and the way in which this art developed throughout the course of its thousand-year-old existence and its aftermath to the end of the 18th century.

The Byzantine heritage

Byzantium is a conception which cannot be confined within the elastic geographical limits of an empire, as it has endured beyond the chronological span of the history of a state. Byzantium always remains alive, not only in the historical memory, but also in the life of modern Hellenism. Among the various Orthodox peoples who inherited the prodigious legacy of civilization bequeathed by the Greek mediaeval empire — it extended over vast areas for over a thousand years — the Greeks have had the privilege to remain in direct contact and actually live, until now, with the still vital essential elements of which the Byzantine world was composed. The Greek language continues to evolve uninterruptedly from the Byzantine, both in the "demotic" and official tongues. The liturgy and other ecclesiastical functions, which are still associated with the most crucial moments in the life of a modern Greek — from the day of his birth to that of his death — are celebrated in the same ecclesiastical tongue, to the accompaniment of the same ecclesiastical chants. The same religious and social customs and habits remain alive; with them too are closely related the works of Byzantine and post-Byzantine art whose roots are deeply implanted in Greek soil. The Byzantine or Byzantine-style icon continues to be an indispensable and highly revered household object. The very existence of Hellenism under foreign domination, for century after century, played an important role in the preservation and survival of these mediaeval traditions.

But the modern way of life, which is constantly and ever more intensively undergoing a levelling process, is increasingly fraying the basic structure of that traditional way of life and alienating men from their origins. A conscious fear of the possible loss of something which is vital to the spiritual and moral nature of the nation has induced enlightened men — not only in Greece, but also in the West

— to concentrate their scholarship on further research into the history of Byzantium and to attempt to recover, conserve and assemble all the proven tokens of Byzantine civilization and its post-Byzantine aftermath. In doing so, they have given priority to the works of Byzantine art.

The expanse of Byzantine art

When we refer to Byzantine art, we mean the art which flourished, above all, in the areas constituting the Byzantine Empire during a long period which lasted from the foundation of its capital in A.D. 330 until its fall in 1453. The actual geographical limits within which Byzantine art spread are considerably wider, for within them must be included areas which were once Byzantine (but not so later), such as the provinces of Ravenna and Sicily, before being conquered by the Lombards and Normans in the 7th and 11th centuries respectively, and the Greek East prior to the Arab conquest in the 7th century. Other areas, such as Crete, Cyprus, the smaller islands of the Aegean and Ionian archipelagoes, remained noteworthy centres of Byzantine art even after their subjection to foreign rule (13th century).

Apart from these areas which were dependencies, in one way or another, of the Byzantine state at different times, one must also take into account the wide sphere of influence penetrated by Byzantine art, to a whole world over which the Orthodox Church held sway: in other words, to those lands of South-Eastern Europe, to Russia and Georgia, where Byzantine artists and authentic works of the official art of Constantinople sowed the seeds from which new shoots sprouted and enabled regional schools to be founded.

Finally, since Byzantine art was closely associated with the fortunes of the Empire, the leading role it played, and the place of honour accorded to it, in a world betwixt East and West, were the natural consequences of the ecumenical authority enjoyed by Byzantium.

Constantinople

Special significance is attached to the epithet "Byzantine" (even if only in a purely conventional sense), for it is of course associated with the name of "Byzantium", a Greek colony at the entrance to the Bosporos. This new city, New Rome, the oecumenic centre and largest city in the world during the Middle Ages, was Constantinople itself; and it was Constantinople that was destined to become the prime factor in the formation of the particular characteristics of Byzantine art. When the capital was transferred by Constantine the Great to the banks of the Bosporos (A.D. 330), the city had no artistic traditions whatsoever; but the entire imperial sphere over which New Rome was mistress already possessed a common artistic language developed in the large Hellenistic cities of the Eastern Mediterranean: Alexandria, Antioch, Ephesos; even Rome itself. Constantinople, at once capital of the Empire and head of the Orthodox Church, did not only absorb and assimilate this quasi-universal artistic language, with all its various nuances, but also formed, fashioned and elaborated it in conformity with the new philosophical views and aesthetic ideas which were in the process of being developed in the capital. These progressively evolving artistic forms, stamped with the authority of authenticity, spread to the periphery in various ways. Plans of churches, for instance, would be despatched by the Emperor to monasteries enjoying his favour, and the carved marbles of Prokonesos would be carried in ships to all the ports of the Mediterranean in order to decorate new churches. Then there were the mosaicists and the painters who were commissioned by the Arab caliphs to decorate their mosques; and the illuminated manuscripts — codices and scrolls — as well as the priceless works of the minor arts executed in the most effective techniques.

The regulating and creative role of a capital of a centralized and basically theocratic state was one of the principal factors which enabled Byzantine art to preserve its fundamental homogeneousness in all its various manifestations, despite the gradual though essential developments it underwent during the course of its life-span, whether in the capital itself or in those places beyond the frontiers of the state where the influence of Constantinople was still predominant. Furthermore, as Byzantine art acquired its unity and style in the Greek environment of Constantinople, it remained stamped, throughout its historical evolution, with the seal of its own origins.

The dual origins of Byzantine art

It is not easy to determine the precise moment of the birth of Byzantine art. Conventionally, it is dated to the time of the foundation of Constantinople — a further indirect recognition of the importance of the role played by the city in the development of Byzantine art. In effect, assimilation and transubstantiation of this universal artistic language, which was of Hellenistic origin, as we have already noted, must have been under way before the foundation of Constantinople. The evidence is not lacking. An iconographic cycle of scenes from the Old and New Testaments, as well as a symbolical medium of the Christian faith, had been formed at an earlier date: in the Catacombs, for instance. Even during the period of the great monarchical states, which preceded the Byzantine, representations of the cycle of imperial iconographies existed. These iconographies possessed a style, at once sober and official, imbued with the grandeur befitting them: a style that was destined to prevail in similar Byzantine representations and to proliferate in those of ecclesiastical iconography.

Besides the classical tradition, with its roots in ancient Greek art, certain anti-classical trends, which emerged in the form of a rough, robust and more popular art and developed in the peripheral provinces of Asia Minor, Syria and Mesopotamia, must also be taken into account. This expressionist art succeeded in becoming an official state art during the Tetrarchy (c. A.D. 300). Some scholars identify this art with a simplified misconception of classical models on the part of craftsmen lacking Greek culture: with, in fact, a so-called democratization of Greek art. Others see in it an artistic trend aiming at an aggressive revival of a somewhat indigenous character. Parallel manifestations may be observed in Sasanian art in Persia (3rd - 7th centuries). Generally speaking, this style is characterized by flat forms with bold outlines, by expressive attitudes and gestures, divorced of any feeling for nobility and elegance, by a preference for two-dimensional representation and an indifference for the real dimensions regulating the relations between human figures. This trend, taken in conjunction with similar expressionistic characteristics, which manifest themselves in varying degrees, reveal a conscious opposition to the classical tradition. The trend does not merely survive, it actually constitutes one of the main determining factors in the formation of a Byzantine Style.

The cyclical recurrence of traditions. Byzantine "philanthropy"

These dual roots were constantly to influence Byzantine art: on the one hand, with the survival or revival of general subjects or special motifs as well as modes of artistic expression; on the other, with a prevailing general disposition in favour of one or another of the tendencies in question.

The classical tradition constitutes, more especially, a living heritage bequeathed by antiquity; it possesses an authentic ring of humanism which does not belong to the closed circles of Atticistic scholars, but is a value of wider significance which saturates Byzantine art and distinguishes it from that of both the West and the East. This humanistic conception of Byzantine art — of whatever period and of whatever trend — becomes intelligible when we comprehend its total devotion to the human form, to its proportions and to the organic relation between its various parts. This conception applies even when the claims of a compositional rhythm and transcendental representation, corresponding more closely to an idea of the intelligible world (which ought to become a tangible one), necessitate certain abstractions which ultimately lead the figurative art to a point beyond the mere imitation of the natural form. This Byzantine *philanthropy* humanized God through the power of sympathy and compassion and deified man by endowing him with a transcendental reality extending far beyond a mere momentary or subjective experience of the world. Even in architecture the dimensions are calculated to the measure of man; this is not only so in small churches; it also applies to those edifices which aim at the grandiose, such as St. Sophia. In the latter one does not feel overwhelmed, as in a Gothic cathedral, by the mass; on the contrary, one feels both surrounded and transported by the grandeur of the enclosed brightly illuminated space, which, in spite of its dimensions, does not diminish one's stature.

The Classical revivals

From time to time, however, the triumph of anti-classical trends would, in its turn, bring about a conscious return to classical models. This kind of renascence — it has in fact been called a "renaissance", whereas the Byzantines themselves termed it a "revival" — often coincided with the accession to the throne of an emperor who may also be the founder of a new dynasty. The tradition followed by the Romans was Hellenistic in origin. In the 1st century A.D. Augustus favoured a return to Praxitelean models — idealized, full of serenity, charm and beauty — in contrast to the realistic-materialistic art of the period. Theodosios the Great (4th century A.D.) put an end to the predominance of provincial concepts which still found expression in the reliefs at the base of his honorific stele erected in Constantinople (known as the Obelisk of Theodosios), in which the figures, depicted frontally, are aligned in successive series. In the 6th century Justinian too, in his general policy aimed at the reestablishment of the Roman Empire, returned to Roman stylistic devices. A similar tendency is observed in the reign of Herakleios (7th century). The love shown by the members of the Macedonian dynasty (9th-10th centuries) for Hellenistic subjects and styles, which is apparent in the preference shown by the Macedonian emperors for carved ivories and illuminated manuscripts executed in the palace workshops, must also derive from the same tradition. There is a return, therefore, not only to unaltered mythological representations and to the medical and pharmaceutical subjects of, among others, Hippokrates and Dioskourides, but also to Byzantine imagery — particularly in the Psalters — rendered in the manner, and by the use of motifs, typical of mythological scenes or episodes from ancient drama. Similar manifestations are observed during the reign of the Komnenoi (11th-12th centuries), as represented by the mosaics at Daphni. Later, during the reign of the Palaiologoi (13th-15th centuries), the return to earlier iconographic and stylistic means of expression acquired a more universal character because it corresponded to a general disposition for emphasis on grace and picturesqueness or dramatic content and lively movement. This periodic revitalization of the classical tradition, even if it originated in aristocratic or exclusively court circles, served as an active incentive for the constant renewal of the wider Hellenistic trends which had never ceased to animate Byzantine art.

Islamic influences

From time to time, however, revivals of the other, the anti-classical, trend were apparent; sometimes in the form of a return to Sasanian decoration (9th-10th centuries) and frequently in a ready acceptance of the influence exercised by contemporary Islamic art, particularly in the field of decorative work and handicrafts. In textiles, in ceramics, in silverware and the goldsmith's craft, even in decorative sculpture, the contacts remained unbroken.

It must, however, be stressed that the dual origins in Byzantine art, which emerge as two parallel traditions, in reality co-exist in close union and frequently influence each other. It may therefore be claimed that they have lost the character attributed to their origins and simply constitute two different means of expression; they may also be apparent in the same work executed by the same artist — even in the same illuminated manuscript — for reasons which are not always easy to verify. This mutual infiltration, as much in the sphere of technique as in that of iconography and style, is an important factor in the maintenance of the basic morphological unity of Byzantine art of all periods; its function is parallel to that of numerous other factors, as well as the intricate structure of Byzantine life, whose unity secured an unbroken continuity and demanded the existence of a fully developed artistic language with a conservative character and a recurring pattern.

The historical framework of Byzantine art

The history of Byzantine art is closely linked with the fortunes of the Empire, and its division into periods, made in the interests of convenience, generally correspond to actual historical periods.

The Early Christian era begins either with the recognition of Christianity as the official religion of the State (313) or with the foundation of the capital (330) and closes with the end of the reign of Justinian (565) or, according to other scholars, whose contention I personally support, with the end of the reign of Herakleios (630). During this period the tradition of a grandiose imperial art of Roman character remained vigorous and unbroken; it therefore coincides with what archaeologists call Late Antiquity. During this period the basic architectural types were also formed, and a new monumental style emerged in painting. The beginning of the Iconoclast period (725-843) is one of extreme importance, for it witnessed the destruction of many works of art, and the development of representational art was arrested as a result of the official attitude regarding the proscription of icon-worship. Religious painting consequently acquired a purely secular or decorative character. This period corresponds with a great internal crisis in the state which is crystallized in the dispute over the significance of the icons.

With the end of Iconoclasm (843) and the rise of the Macedonian dynasty (861) begins the Middle Byzantine period which lasted until 1204. For the first time the great capital fell and remained in the hands of the Crusaders. In 1261 Michael Palaiologos, the self-styled "New Constantine", ushered in a new period; a painful one for the fortunes of the Empire, but an important one as regards the fortunes of an art which, with noteworthy achievements, made use of new forms of expression, always returning to, and making selections from, older models of a kind which suited its own particular character. Byzantine art did not come to an end with the fall of Constantinople in 1453. It remained alive in the Cretan school of painting and in woodcarving; it manifested itself in the grand architectural edifices of the monasteries raised on Mt.Athos and elsewhere, in metal-work and, in a general way, in numerous sophisticated works of the minor arts, whose creators, after the disappearance of the great melting-pot constituted by the capital, moved to the peripheral areas of the former Empire.

Architecture

It is now time to examine the various categories of Byzantine works of art.
In architecture there are the large edifices of the Graeco-Roman period, with the modifications

9

effected by the demands of the new official religion both as regards its ideological presentation and the practice of the new faith. The main types of religious edifices — basilicas, centralized buildings, domed basilicas, octagonal and other constructions planned in such a way as to conform to their particular function (churches, martyria, baptisteries, etc) — were formulated in the Early Christian period. New architectural features, such as the transverse aisle of the basilica and the dome raised by means of different combinations of methods for supporting it, were created. The church was furthermore adorned with the Holy Table, with a *ciborium*, episcopal throne, *synthronon*, *ambon*, altar screen, closure panels, etc. All these architectural features were executed in carved polychrome marbles and decorated with lavish materials (sometimes with precious stones) or covered with silver, gold and enamel. The numerous columns — frequently taken from ancient temples — were crowned with elaborately worked capitals which supported the elegant arches. In poorer districts the floors of churches were paved with decorative mosaics, whereas more lavish constructions were adorned with huge plaques of matching marbles so that the veins formed decorative designs. The walls were covered with framed marbles, the barrel vaults, arches and domes with mosaics whose gold ground reflected the light which filled the church from numerous windows. The whole of the splendid illuminated interior, of whatever architectural type, corresponded to a microcosm, to a symbolic picture of the universe which must be provided by the church.

For historical reasons, Byzantine architecture after the 6th century never again possessed the majestic forms which distinguished it in the Early Christian era; it never again had the same wide variety of types nor did the abundance of solutions to architectural problems exist any longer.

The type subsequently destined to prevail was the cruciform church with dome. It developed slowly, with a constant attempt on the part of architects to preserve the unity of the large dome-covered central space which tended to break away from the four supports of the dome, whether pilasters or columns.

With the achievement of the solution of the constructional problem of supporting the dome with lighter buttresses, or even with their total removal in the octagonal type evolved in the 10th-11th centuries, and with the consequent elongation of the arms of the cross, the pattern of the cross itself and the organic structure of the building became far more apparent in the roof and exterior surfaces. The clarity of the design and the harmonious proportions now matched a classical conception of form. The interior surfaces were covered with precious materials, marbles, mosaics, wall-paintings. The exterior also became more elaborate, the surfaces being either plastically executed or consisting of perfectly wrought masonry, embellished with lavish brick decoration.

Sculpture

After the 6th century the carving of statues in the round ceased; sculptured reliefs, however, continued to be executed in abundance, especially as component parts of architectural features. Some sculptors were faithful to classical traditions; others borrowed examples from neighbouring Eastern countries. In the use of this two-dimensional technique sculptors frequently tried to imitate the technique of enamels by resorting to the use of coloured materials or even painting. In the smaller plaques of ivory and later of steatite (a cheaper material which replaced the more expensive ivory) a refined technique of low relief was evolved. The representations were greatly influenced by the classical tradition, irrespective of whether they possessed a secular or religious character.

Monumental painting. Mosaics. Wall-paintings

In monumental painting — whether mosaic or wall-painting — Byzantine artists endeavoured to fulfil the requirements of the new religion: namely, to glorify the triumph of the Church in pictorial symbols, to narrate the history of the Old and New Testaments to the ignorant and create representations with an authentic and orthodox dogmatic significance.

The two elaborate techniques involved in mosaic and wall-painting were inherited by Byzantine artists, together with corresponding artistic styles, from earlier periods.

A large number of mosaics of the Early Christian period, in which cycles of cosmological representations are often encountered, are preserved in pavements. To these are related the "mural" mosaics, which are superior in quality from an artistic standpoint, such as those in the Rotunda of St. George, Hosios David, St. Demetrios and the *Acheiropoietos* (all in Thessalonike), at Ravenna, in the remote Monastery of St. Catherine on Mt. Sinai and elsewhere. An official style, characterized by figures depicted frontally standing in front of buildings, with the emphasis on the portrait-like aspect, and by drapery resembling the flutings of columns prevails, in varying degrees, in these mosaics. Here one may trace the gradual transformation of Hellenistic portraiture and iconography into the transcendental icon, with the eventual disappearance of three-dimensional space, accompanied by a trend towards an inorganic articulation of the figures and a tendency for the face to be depicted with large eyes. This transformation took place between the 5th and 7th centuries. The same style is encountered in contemporary wall-paintings, many of which are in Rome — executed by craftsmen from the East — in the islands and elsewhere. It is important to stress the fact that indications of certain contemporary trends are also encountered in churches of the first importance, such as St. Sophia and the Holy Apostles in Constantinople, which possessed lavish but non-figurative decorations (crosses, etc.).

After the Iconoclast period (725-843) the chief trends in Byzantine painting, which had existed in diffused form at an earlier date, assumed a definite form; these trends were furthermore apparent in imperial circles, as one may observe in the decoration executed in St. Sophia during the 9th century and later. The entire mosaic decoration in churches, such as that in St. Sophia at Thessalonike, Hosios Loukas, Nea Moni on Chios, and Daphni, represents trends which are basically in opposition to each other: on the one hand, we have a return to classical models; on the other, the avoidance of any reference to antiquity. Features deriving from different trends, always of a high artistic quality and of outstanding technical perfection, coexist in a single strikingly dramatic art. The wall-paintings of the period, many examples of which are to be found in, among other places, Thessalonike, Kastoria, Achris, Cyprus and at Hosios Loukas, reveal the monumental character of these large compositions with imposing figures rendered in most impressive manner. By the end of the 12th century, however, this style was to lead the way to the adoption of a somewhat affected one, known as a linear mannerist style, in which the figures become extremely elongated and are clad in light clinging garments with elaborate draperies.

The 13th century was a critical period for monumental painting which now followed a new road. Works of art were executed in the smaller court centres of the dismembered Empire and neighbouring Balkan states. A reaction to the mannerist style of the 12th century is encountered in wide tranquil compositions in which the desire for the expression of a kind of epic grandeur reached its zenith at Sopoçani (1265) and in the mosaics in the *Paregoretissa* at Arta (1295), where the very free use of a painter's means are apparent. A style, full of liveliness, expressed in a highly dramatic manner, with the depiction of plethoric figures which often possess a definitely violent character, flourished around 1300. This style has been called "Macedonian", because some of the finest specimens are encountered on Mt. Athos and in the Macedonian areas. At the same time painting of high quality was being executed in Constantinople, as also elsewhere. Although somewhat academic in character, it did not lack elegance of design or distinction of colour. Despite certain variations, this style lasted until the end; it was accompanied by a tendency to diminish the monumental aspect and replace it with an episodic often charming narrative quality. After the fall of Constantinople the style continued to animate the works of the artists of the Cretan school during the 16th and 17th centuries, but it became more austere in character and the compositions tended to be more classical. Italian influences are also evident.

Portative icons

The portative icon is one of the purest Byzantine creations throughout all the periods, in the course of which it preserves the unmistakable mark of its origins in ancient portraiture. The earliest and best examples (6th century), executed in the old technique of encaustic painting, are in the Monastery of St. Catherine on Mt. Sinai. In the succeeding centuries, following the Iconoclast period, the meaning of the icon, which is itself an as it were active participant in the divine grace enjoyed by the saint whose portrait it represents, because of its likeness to him, is further established, in terms of neoplatonic theory.

As regards style, the painting in the portative icon follows the actual development of painting in general; it is, however, associated, according to its size, function and subject, with either monumental painting or the art of the miniature. The gradual development of the screen of the altar into a tall wide iconostasis, with its iconographic programme, which is gradually formed and stabilized after the 11th century, together with the frequent repetition of archetypes of famous miraculous icons, also contributed to the flowering of the portative icon.

Miniatures

The method adopted in the execution of the illuminated manuscript — whether in the form of a scroll or codex — is continued, in conformity with the ancient Greek conception, in the art of the miniature. The illustrations transfer the narrative to the sphere of the visual arts and thus become more explicit. The Old and New Testaments are consequently illustrated and the various elements of the miniature — the shapes, attitudes and gestures, the depiction of the garments — derive from the illustration of ancient texts, as well as from representations from Graeco-Judaic monuments.

During the Byzantine period the illustration of liturgical books underwent a great diffusion, particularly in the case of Books of Gospels; sometimes it is confined to depictions of the four Evangelists; sometimes too, it may include the Twelve Feasts of the liturgical calendar. The composition is more carefully studied, less descriptive, and the miniature often becomes a model for a representation of larger dimensions, for a portative icon or a work of monumental painting. The liturgical books also include Psalters, *Menologia* (accompanied by scenes from the lives and martyrdoms of the saints pertaining to each month) and, above all, the more rare liturgical scrolls. The miniatures develop on parallel lines with the portative icon, with which they are stylistically closely related.

It is also possible to study the survival and revival of the various traditions in the art of the miniature. Some lavish parchment codices have been preserved which were undoubtedly executed in the court *scriptoria;* in them one may detect, with absolute assurance, the source of each revivifying trend in the centres of high culture.

THE BYZANTINE MUSEUM: The building

The Byzantine Museum, one of the most important in the country, was not a feature of the Athenian scene until 1930. Its establishment is owed to the late George Sotiriou, who succeeded through his own efforts, favoured by the general political and cultural climate of the times, to have at his disposal an assembly of buildings, until then occupied by a military service of secondary importance. The original buildings had been commissioned by the Duchesse de Plaisance, a romantic and aristocratic French lady, in 1840. At the time, the site lay on the outskirts of the new capital, on the banks of the Ilisos, whose river-bed is now covered by a broad thoroughfare serving all that part of the city which has spread far beyond the Duchess' former country house. The place was called *Ilissia* (perhaps an allusion to the Parisian Elysées), the front entrance being, as it is today, on Vasilissis Sophias Avenue, but with the main view on the Ilisos and Hymettos.

The group of buildings was designed by Stamatios Kleanthis, one of the few oustanding Greek architects of the period, who provided the main edifice with the simple and elegant style of a Florentine Renaissance mansion.

It was not an easy task to convert a private residence into a museum of mainly religious art, with the emphasis on its didactic character. The contribution of another architect, Aristoteles Zachos, proved to be of considerable value in effecting a successful architectural arrangement of, above all, the ground floor which was intended to give the impression of a model of the three types of churches prevailing in the Greek world: the Early Christian basilica, the Byzantine cruciform church with dome and the post-Byzantine single-space religious building. Furthermore, the collections allocated to other parts of the museum had to be arranged in such a manner as to facilitate a logical classification of objects.

The museum was avowedly intended, in the words of George Sotiriou, "to provide a picture of the evolution of the art developed in the Greek world from the close of antiquity to the time of the deliverance of the Greek Nation from the Turkish yoke." The assembled collections intended for display in the new museum did in effect correspond to this wide scope; for the most part they consisted of works of mediaeval art in the Helladic area, although some of the objects cannot, in all cases, be said to the confined to these geographical limits.

The collections

One of the large basic collections consisted of numerous marble sculptrures found on the Acropolis and in various ruined or demolished churches in the Athens area and formerly assembled by the Archaeological Service in the "Theseion". A second collection included a few pieces of wall-paintings which had been removed at various times from demolished churches in Athens, Delphi and Atalante, as well as some impressive icons of the Palaiologan period and gold-thread embroideries from the Thessalonike area. A large collection of icons, manuscripts, liturgical objects, vestments, etc., came from the Christian Archaeological Society formed in 1884 by a number of distinguished amateurs, among whom the moving spirit was George Lambakis. An enthusiastic admirer of Christian art, he succeeded, over a period of several decades, in acquiring donations, in publishing a *Deltion* (bulletin) containing valuable information and in photographing the monuments he saw in his frequent travels to remote localities.

After the Asia Minor disaster of 1922 the uprooted refugees brought a further collection of valuable ecclesiastical relics from their homelands. A selection of fine liturgical objects was shared between the Byzantine and Benaki Museum. Of foreing provenance is a small collection of Coptic inscriptions and so-called Coptic textiles presented to the museum by Anthony Benaki with a view to giving visitors an opportunity to form an impression of this art.

When the Byzantine Museum was first founded in 1914 the collections were housed in the unsuitable and wholly inadequate accommodation provided by a basement in the megaron of the Academy. When transferred to the restored edifice by the Ilisos they were displayed in the halls of the three wings and in the large court which was transformed in such a way as to resemble a monastic one, with cypress trees and a *phiale*. Later a fountain was added and a plane tree planted.

New donations were made and new legacies inherited as a result of the prestige acquired by the museum after its establishment at the present site. The collection of portative icons was thus enriched with the acquisition of the private collections of Christianos Lampikis, Professor John Katsaras, George Makkas, Melissidis, etc. The museum also continued to be enriched with murals detached from the walls of churches, sculptures from the collection of various scattered antiquities, objects (particularly glassware and ceramics) uncovered in the course of excavations, icons from confiscated antiquities, as well as other objects obtained by means of purchases or from donations made by private individuals.

In order to house all these acquisitions, both old and new, and exhibit them properly it was found necessary in 1951 to build another spacious well-lit hall in the east wing.

The foundation of a Central Laboratory of Conservation (of wall-paintings, mosaics and icons) in 1963 was a landmark in the history of the museum. The members of the laboratory were responsible for the preservation of wall-paintings in hundreds of churches throughout Greece, for the restoration of mosaics on the walls and floors of churches. Many fragments of Byzantine wall-paintings had to be detached from walls and removed for restoration to the Byzantine Museum, where some of them are now exhibited. A special apartment was reserved for the laboratories in which the icons in the museum underwent the various processes required for conservation, and the activities of the Central Laboratory were extended to include the conservation of monuments as far afield as Cyprus and Palestine and of wall-paintings and icons in the Monastery of St. Catherine on Mt. Sinai.

Early Christian works (4th-7th century)

The Byzantine Museum is perhaps the only one exclusively devoted to works of Byzantine and post-Byzantine art. The museum owes its regional character to the fact that since its foundation, it has included representative works of art of the Byzantine era and the age of the Turkish rule as developed within the confines of the present Greek state. That is why the collections possess such a pronounced local character. This is a very pertinent point. For it should be recalled that Northern Greece with Thessalonike as its centre fell within the area subject to the immediate influence of the Capital, while the rest of Greece south of Mt. Olympos was a Byzantine province with somewhat independent historical fortunes determined by its position in the Mediterranean. Here, along the limitless shores, in the numerous islands of the Aegean and Ionian Seas, in the large and famous ancient cities — Corinth, Athens, Megara, Sparta, Argos, Boiotian Thebes, Phthiotic Thebes and Gortyna in Crete, among others — life followed its own course.

Judging from the great number of large ruined churches and from the high quality of their decoration uncovered in the course of excavations, one must conclude that the whole area now consisting of modern Greece must have been a prosperous one during the Early Christian period. The objects from Thessalonike, Asia Minor and elsewhere, exhibited in the ante-chamber of the ground floor of the museum, were fashioned in a superb technique, betraying the catholicity of their style. The next hall, which is in the form of a three-aisled basilica, gives the visitor an idea of the disposition of a church of this type, with the low screen of the sanctuary, the *synthronon* and throne, the Holy Table, *ambon* and closure panels. Early Christian sculptures — offering tables, closure panels from the Ilisos basilica and other churches — have been assembled in this hall. (Pieces from the mosaic floor of the Ilisos basilica are displayed in the west gallery of the court). The funerary group of Orpheus (fig. 2) strikes a different note. The seated figure of the harpist is surrounded by an arched frame consisting of beasts, birds and other animals (both real and fantastical) disposed in successive series so that the empty spaces between them and between the frame and the central figure create hollows which give the impression that the entire composition has been executed in the manner of open-work technique. In spite of the plastic modelling of each figure, the entire group conveys an impression, heightened by the deeply incised folds of drapery, of a flat representation. The modelling is a typical example of the period (*c*. A.D. 400), but the Christian character of the representation (possibly a symbolical figure of Christ?) remains doubtful.

To the same period of flourishing belongs the "Mytilene treasure" (figs. 27-29): a hoard of gold, silver and bronze objects, as well as gold coins, which was found in 1951 at the locality of Krategos, where they had been hidden by persons in fear of some Arab raid. The owners, it would appear, never had the opportunity of returning and recovering them. The gold objects consist of jewellery (fig. 27): three necklaces with open-work decoration, earrings, two belts, bracelets, buckles, rings. The technique, of Roman origin, is evolved, and the craftsmen were obviously aiming at the creation of precious objects that would convey an impression of considerable brilliance. It is not strange that the decoration occasionally bears obviously Christian traces, for the gold coins with which they were found are of the period of the Emperors Phokas (602-610) and Herakleios (613-629/30).

To the same period clearly belong the silver objects from the same treasure, all of which are *pentasphragista:* that is to say, stamped with the five official seals of the controller of the quality of silver. The dish is simply decorated with a cross surrounded by a tendril with ivy leaves (fig. 28). All the objects are decorated with niello, i.e. darkened silver. On the hollow object with a handle, called a *trulla,* a nude female figure and four youthful ones are incised on the wide handle and lip respectively (fig. 29). The decorative subject must derive from some revival of pagan worship in Late Antiquity; but the linear incisions reveal the various transformations that this kind of art had undergone by the 7th century.

Art of the Middle Byzantine period in Greece (8th-12th century)

From the mid-7th to mid-9th century pestilence, Arab raids on the coasts and hostile incursions from the north caused widespread devastation and the depopulation of the maritime areas. The country was only able to breathe again when Crete was liberated (961) and the Bulgar threat effectively removed. It must be stressed, however, that Greece's economic means were at a very much lower ebb than they had been during the Early Christian period. The collection of marble pieces of architectural decoration of the post-Iconoclast period in the museum is nevertheless a very rich one. The pieces include a large number of door-frames, lintels, closure panels and architraves of screens, as well as some rare large marble icons with the Virgin in an attitude of prayer carved in relief. Although possessing the general artistic characteristics of the period, all this material, carved in Pentelic marble, must represent the fruits of labour of workshops in the Attica-Boiotia area. Let us take a look at a closure panel representing the old Eastern theme of the Tree of Life in a symmetrical but dynamic composition with two lions rising to bite the tree, their hind-paws treading on its roots whence water gushes forth (fig. 4). The shallow relief, the stylized manes, the *horror vacui* shown by the sculptor would in themselves suffice to betray the Eastern provenance of the subject and style, were it not further verified by the pseudo-Cufic inscription on the two lateral sides of the frame. Other similar inscriptions in the form of decorative features, whose provenance cannot be disputed, are to be found on other pieces in the museum which, in many cases, formed part of buildings and reliefs of the 10th and 11th centuries in Southern Greece, and provide evidence of a temporary change in taste in favour of Islamic art of the Eastern Mediterranean. The same change is evident in another closure panel with the extremely ancient motif of a lion about to tear its prey to pieces (fig. 6). The execution is more rough, the rendering of the relief more flat, but the fact that the composition is equally dynamic in conception underlines the difference between the piece in question and the Eastern models. Sculptures with similar subjects decorate the walls of the Church of St. Eleutherios (otherwise known as the *Gorgoepekoos* or Little Metropolis). These were removed from earlier Athenian churches. Double knotted crosses decorate other closure panels, like the one with the metrical dedicatory inscription (fig. 5) from the demolished Athenian Church of St. John of Mangoutis. The manner in which the eagles are depicted within medallions, even though in heraldic attitudes and rendered with a certain academic plasticity, is an indication of the different origins of this kind of sculpture.

The sculptures we have examined so far are all of Athenian provenance. An interesting piece representing three Apostles, James Alphaius, Philip and Luke (fig. 3) comes from Thessalonike which remained in direct contact with Constantinople. The somewhat short standing figures, depicted frontally, are accompanied by vertical incised inscriptions with impeccably designed majuscules. An interesting technique, known as *champ-levé*, has been used. The outlines of the figures are drawn with the removal of interior surfaces, whereas the folds of the garments — this applies to all three figures — are indicated by fine projecting edges. The hollows are filled with mastic wax on which the draperies with the many folds, the faces and large hands are painted. It is clear that the technique used in the depiction of flat figures and the separately painted stains is, in this instance, an imitation of the *cloisonné* enamels and, in painting, of the one applied to portative icons. This valuable plaque, which should be dated to the 10th rather than the 11th century, must have formed part of the lavish decoration of a marble screen (of a length exceeding 4.50 metres) and constituted a section of the usual screen architrave of the period representing the Great *Deesis* (the three main figures with the twelve Apostles).

The Frankish occupation and the Palaiologan period (1204-1453)

The brilliant period of the 11th and 12th centuries, which is represented by monuments of such superior quality as Hosios Loukas and Daphni, together with other beautiful churches of the Helladic school, was followed by the Frankish occupation which began in 1204 and came to an end with the Turkish conquest in 1456. Churches continued to be raised during this period and their walls to be painted; but they were of smaller dimensions, built of cheaper materials and more scattered as a result of a decentralizing tendency which caused many people to dwell in private family domains. An idea of monumental painting in Attica and the islands during the 13th century can be obtained from pieces of wall-paintings detached from the walls of churches and exhibited in the museum.

The tall slender figure of a young deacon (fig. 8), St. Stephen (?), is painted on a narrow pilaster beside the hierarchs on the altar of a new ruined church at Oropos. The striking facial features, the heroic character, the firm outlines and the modelling rendered by means of the use of both warm and cool colour tones, relate this wall-painting to similar ones of the mid-13th century in Euboia and at Kranidi which we have reason to attribute to an Athenian school of painting. At Kranidi the paintings are signed by a certain John of Athens and dated 1244.

Paintings in the islands under Frankish domination underwent a different development. A conch of the apse of a church at Lathreno, Naxos, has been detached from the wall (fig. 7). Its poor state of preservation indicates that it might have suffered total destruction had it not been removed. The large central figure of Christ is out of proportion with the two flanking figures in the *Deesis*, those of the Virgin and St. John the Baptist, which are preserved intact. These wall-paintings provide evidence of the way in which the repercussions of new trends in Constantinople were felt in the occupied provinces, as well as the manner in which Western influences affected Byzantine taste.

The large mosaic icon of the Virgin and child, *"the Glykophilousa"* from Triglia in Bithynia, which is one of the outstanding relics brought by the refugees in 1922, should be assigned to a slightly later date: namely, the early 14th century (fig. 1). The size of the icon, as well as that of the tesserae, indicates that the work was still closely related to the kind of art whose origins lay in monumental mosaics, whereas other outstanding mosaic icons possess the dimensions of miniatures. Furthermore, as the icon bears the inscription Η ΕΠΙΣΚΕΨΙΣ, it must be a reproduction of some miraculous icon of the *Glykophilousa,* in which the Virgin holds the Child in her right arm (the subject was also rendered in the remarkable Virgin of Vladimir in the 12th century). In the Byzantine Museum icon the fleshy luminous faces and the bulky bodies, which are characteristic of a contemporary trend, have been rendered in a closed condensed composition with soft outlines. The bright colours with the abundant gold lights conceal certain weaknesses in the design.

Icons

Of all the exhibits in the Byzantine Museum the portative icons, with their wide range of geographical provenance, provide the most comprehensive picture of the different styles.

The Crucifixion (provenance: Northern Greece) is depicted on one side of a double-sided icon, whose history is best summarized in its lack of homogeneity (fig. 15). In the 13th century the principal figures were repainted over the early icon of the 9th century which possessed flat and linear features, such as the angels and the stars. Grief and suffering are expressed in a striking but restrained manner which matches the simplicity of the colour scheme and composition.

Another double-sided icon comes from the same area, namely Kastoria. St. George is depicted full-size, carved on the wood of the icon which is framed by little painted scenes from the saint's life and martyrdom (fig. 11). The wood relief, the stiff and awkward attitude of the figure, the nimbus executed in relief and the shape of the shield betray Frankish influences of Romanesque origin. The expressionist technique used in the small scenes of the frame recall miniatures painted at the time of the Frankish kingdoms of Jerusalem and Cyprus. The prolonged cohabitation of peoples in various areas of the Eastern Mediterranean resulting from the Frankish occupation raised the enduring problem of reciprocal exchange of influences which are not always easy to verify. The large icon of Christ (fig. 14), for instance, which may have come from St. Sophia in Thessalonike, is rendered distinctive by two features: by the broad and ugly face, which is in complete contrast to the usual type of idealized Christ, and by the affectedly realistic light and shade effects which give the nimbus an unusual plasticity, as in the relief of the nimbus of St. George (fig. 11). This ugliness — the words of the prophet, "and when we shall see him *there is* no beauty that we should desire him" (Isiah, 53, 2) are not inappropriate here — reflects a clearly anti-classical trend, although the execution is of high quality; moreover the Western-type nimbus may even suggest the origins of this anti-classical tendency. The icon of the Virgin holding the Child from Thessalonike is not alien to this tendency. The serious and aristocratic physiognomy of the Mother of God possesses strikingly individual features, while the figure of the Child, with the high forehead and expression of displeasure concentrated in the disproportionately plump face, as well as the oblique glance and the awkward attitude, does not seem to be in contact with the Mother. Peculiarities of this kind, already observed in the icon of Christ from Thessalonike, would have been inconceivable before 1300; they are typical of a spiritual and artistic movement of the early 14th century which did not possess a particularly regional quality.

The Classical revival

The opposite trend, which remained faithful to the so-called classical tradition, is represented in several outstading icons from the important centres, including the well known one of the Archangel Michael "the *Megas Taxiarches*" (fig. 12). The fine youthful figure is well set up, with the "cast shadow" across the neck, the delicately elaborated drapery with the deep gold lights conveying an impression of something infinitely precious, and the black band, a symbol of authority. Crowned by a lavish arrangement of the hair, the noble face combines the gentle quality of a girl with the serious air of an ephebe; it thus reflects an idealized serene beauty which is full of warm humanity and high moral character. The exceptional artistic quality, taken in conjunction with certain specific features, indicate that the icon is of Constantinopolitan provenance and should be dated after the mid-14th century — or possibly slightly later.

The superb Crucifixion from Thessalonike belongs to about the same period and is in the same tradition (fig. 17). Lacking all narrative elements, the three-figured composition retains its monumental character. The three figures, each one concentrated and isolated within the space of the icon, are related to each other by the harmonious rhythm of attitudes and gestures expressing a grief shared in common. The figure on the Cross is just slightly relaxed, its curve being repeated in the sturdy body of St. John, whereas the Virgin, tall and slender, wrapped in a *maphorion,* stands erect as a column, her attitude and gestures serving as a counterpoise to those of St. John which originate from ancient gravestones. The exceptional height of the figures introduces a new element into the icon. Moreover, the figures are made to appear even taller by the low horizon of the houses of Jerusalem and the diffused light which just permits reflections to fall on the soft folds of drapery and on the nude body on the Cross. The simple colours graduate between a range of brown and gold on which a limpid blue casts a glow.

The nobility of the attitude of the young Daniel depicted in motion as he worships, with a large red cloak thrown elegantly over his shoulders, and the fine workmanship enable us to attribute the icon of the prophet in the den of lions to the same tradition (fig. 16). The prophet Habbakuk, depicted in small scale, is led by an archangel as he proceeds to offer nourishment to Daniel who is now in disgrace.

The large gold-thread *Epitaphios* from Thessalonike (fig. 38), one of the most striking examples of a series of gold-thread works of the Palaiologan era is also assigned to a period associated with a new flowering of the arts. It was designed by an outstanding artist of the early 14th century. Dogmatic ideas are dramatically expressed in three scenes, whereas the perfection of the technical execution, together with a judicious feeling for detail rendered by the use of a variety of precious materials, indicate the high degree of skill attained by the needleworkers, who may well have been noble ladies.

The arts after the fall of Constantinople. Cretan icons

After the fall of Constantinople icon painting continued to occupy the predominant place in the religious art of the Orthodox world, and Greek icons did not cease to be held up as examples of dogmatic orthodoxy and artistic faith in the great Byzantine tradition. The Hospitality of Abraham (fig. 21) is an outstanding example of the art which flourished in the large cities of Crete, the most important centre, where painting, with its attachment to the best Palaiologan models, continued to be of high quality. In this symbolic depiction of the Holy Trinity, features of common everyday life, such as the three young people partaking of a repast, are blurred and the icon acquires the air of an other-worldly representation, as in the case of the Constantinopolitan icon of the Palaiologan period with the same subject in the Benaki Museum. In the Byzantine Museum piece, however, the figures have grown larger and advanced into the foreground, filling the entire space, so that the buildings in the background have lost their importance. The entire composition is subjected to a geometric conception, the influence of which is observed in the disposition of the drapery: the soft and pliant folds have been succeeded by angular forms. An additional feature provided by the aristocratic nobility of the figures and their attitudes enables us to obtain an idea of the main characteristics of Cretan painting of the 15th-16th centuries.

Painters in the Byzantine tradition possessed a particular ability to render the venerable figures of the chief protagonists of the Christian faith in its most ascetic and idealized aspects. The figure of St. Anthony, a very popular with painters, was a subject that greatly attracted them in the exercise of this lofty artistic medium (fig. 20). The austere and tormented face, illuminated by only a few rays of light, the rhythmic folds of drapery which emphasize the extremely tall silhouette and register the movement of the legs, are an expression of the nobility of the ascetic ideal.

Another of the Byzantine icon painter's ideals finds expression in the depiction of female saints martyred in the first flush of their youth, like that wise young princess, St. Catherine (fig. 19). Indications of the ideal of feminine beauty most favoured during the different periods are observed in this kind of icon. An actual physiognomical type is apparent here, fairly common even at present in various parts of Greece. Other characteristics of Cretan painting of the 15th-16th centuries consist of bright colours, a faultless technique employed in the vigorous modelling and the accurate rendering of minor details in dress and ornament which betray Italian influences.

A feeling for maternal tenderness is shown by the Cretan painter Angelos (15th c.) in an not unknown but nevertheless unusual type of the Virgin holding the Child, the *Brephokratousa* (fig. 18). The attitude of the Child, nestling in the Virgin's affectionate embrace, is awkward; but the fact that everything remains in a certain abstract atmosphere is a considerable achievement, which may be observed in other works too, on the part of the Cretan painter.

The icon decorates the large iconostasis of the church (fig. 26); but it can also be interpreted as an expression of individual worship, of personal gratitude, as in the case of the icon dedicated by Capetan Ardavanis to the Virgin of the Venetians who rescued him from a shipwreck (fig. 23). The dramatic scene, represented in the summary but lively manner of Cretan painters, is set on a seashore near the Kourtzoula islets where the battle of Lepanto (Naupaktos) was fought.

In other parts of Greece, outside Crete and the areas in which Cretan painting was diffused, icons and wall-paintings continued to be executed. Cretan artists were commissioned to carry out the painted decoration of the large monasteries on Mt. Athos, at Meteora and elsewhere; but native painters, generally peasants, continued to practise their hereditary and traditional art in smaller churches. Their works, rendered in their own simpler manner, are not uninfluenced by Cretan iconography. The triptych (fig. 22), which must come from Central Greece, represents the Transfiguration on the central panel, the Tree of Jesse and the Vine, two corresponding symbolical representations from the Old and New Testaments, on the left and right panels respectively. The whole work, with the decorative rendering of the symmetrical trees, the brightness of the colours, possess the quality of a handicraftsman's perfectionist work.

Popular painting in the 18th century

A similar but more authentically popular mode of expression is observed in the paintings detached from the walls of the church in the old village of Kastri which was demolished in order to enable the excavation of the ancient Gymnasium of Delphi to be carried out. One of the works, dated to 1751, represents an old monk in a boat, while large sea monsters — the "dragons of the sea" of the Psalter — emerge out of the turbulent waters and belch forth the members of the victims they have devoured on the Day of Judgement (fig. 10). The artist's indifference to the scale of the monsters in relation to reality is evident. Another wall-painting of the same period, detached from the wall of a ruined church at Atalante, represents St. James the Persian (fig. 9), whose exotic apparel displays an attractive colourfulness.

The *Galaktotrophousa* (The Virgin suckling the Child), which is distinguished by an individual kind of realism corresponding to contemporary fashion (fig. 24), is the subject chosen by the monkish painter Makarios from Galatista in the Chalcidike. The type of the Virgin suckling the Child is one of the oldest in Christian iconography, but, a certain prudery inhibited painters from repeating it frequently. The accuracy of a handicraftsman's skill is evident in the rendering of the adornments and nimbuses — an indication that painting has passed into the sphere of handicrafts.

Popular painting in the 19th century inherited the technique and basic principles of hagiography, which in itself had already become a popular art, as one may observe in the charming didactic picture of the blind Eros and the Sirens (fig. 25). The work dated 1825 is by a humble priest and hagiographer from the island of Siphnos.

Minor arts

The museum also contains lavish collections of vestments, *Epitaphioi* (gold-embroidered veils carried in procession on Good Friday) and other liturgical objects representative of the handicrafts, often executed in numerous varied techniques and possessing a high degree of perfection (figs. 30-39). In accordance with their provenance and the period in which they were executed these objects reflect Byzantine survivals, as well as Persian and Western influences. Of the many centres of handicrafts, the most important were in Epeiros, the islands, Asia Minor and Constantinople, as well as in numerous monasteries.

The technical skill and good taste shown by the artists of the Byzantine world, preserved in the unbroken tradition of the Hellenic diaspora, still survive in all their vigour and are constantly undergoing rejuvenation. This too constitutes a direct link with Byzantium.

1. Mosaic icon of the Virgin and Child, 'The Episkepsis'. Provenance: Bithynia. 14th century.

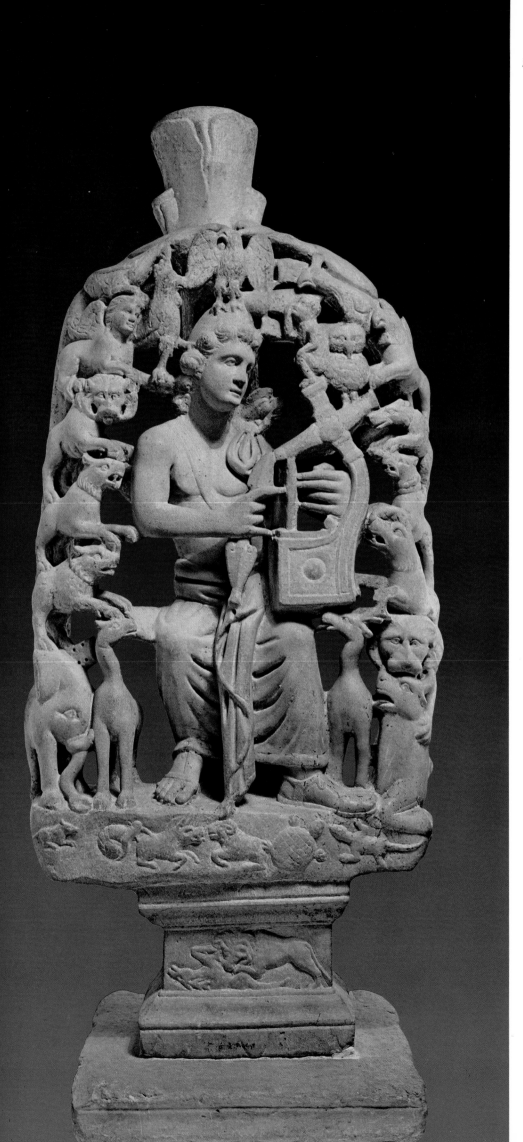

2. *Funerary stele. 4th-5th century. Orpheus, playing on his lyre, fascinates the animals (real and imaginary) which surround him. Relief depicting hunting scene on the base. The group must possess some symbolical meaning associated with immortality.*

3. *Plaque depicting three apostles. Provenance: Thessalonike. The work must have formed part of a marble screen of the 10th-11th century. Screens had developed into one of the most lavish features decorating the interior of contemporary churches.*

4,6. *Marble closure panels from a screen of the 9th-10th century, with the extremely ancient subjects of confronted animals (No. 4) and animals in combat (No. 6), which must have lost their symbolical meaning and were probably a survival from Iconoclast thematology.*

5. *The Victory cross, a Christian symbol of the 9th-10th century with an apotropaic meaning, was commonly carved on closure panels.*

3

4   5   6

7. *Wall-painting from apsidal conch with the Deesis theme. Provenance: Lathreno, Naxos. 13th century. Below: bishops conducting the liturgy.*

8. *Wall-painting detached from wall of ruined church at Oropos. Early 13th century. A tall slender young deacon is clad in a white 'sticharion'. In his left hand, covered by a red encheirion (cloth), he holds a tall gold incense box.*

9. *Wall-painting depicting St. James the Persian. The strange type of the Eastern saint, developed by 16th century Cretan painters, is repeated in the 18th century, but with simpler means. Provenance: demolished church at Atalante.*

10. *Wall-painting from a demolished church at Delphi (1751). A fantastical scene with a boat painted with realistic exactitude.*

7

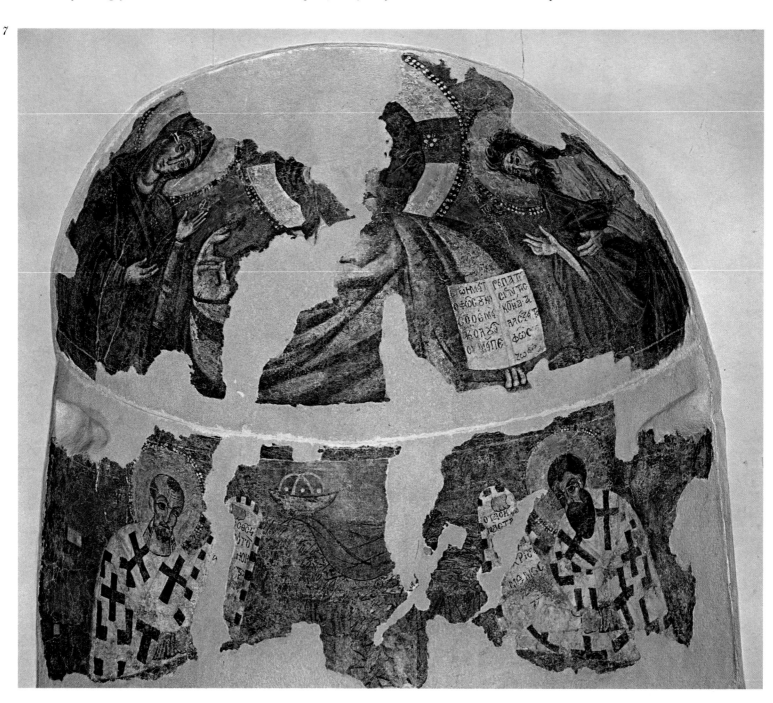

9

10

11. Icon of St. George in painted relief (a somewhat rare technique in the Byzantine world). The little donor at the saint's feet is clothed in Frankish dress. 13th century. Provenance: Kastoria area.

12. The 14th century icon of the Archangel Michael must have formed part of a set of five or seven icons on the upper tier of an iconostasis including the Deesis, as indicated by the three letters on the globe.

13. *Icon of the Virgin and Child. c. 1300. The personal features of the faces reveal a particular trend in Palaiologan painting.*
14. *Large icon of Christ, representative of a high quality anti-classical trend of the early 14th century. Provenance: Thessalonike.*
15. *The Crucifixion. The angels and stars are of a 9th century layer, whereas the main figures are typical of the 13th.*
16. *The prophet Daniel. The subject, rare in portative icons, is depicted here in the elegant manner of Palaiologan painting.*
17. *The Crucifixion. Outstanding work of Palaiologan painting, from Thessalonike.*

18

19

20

21

ΟΝ ...ΗΤΕΔΒΡΔΜ ΗΟΖΩ
ΧΙΒ ΙCΤΙΔΔΟC ΦΝΕΡΓΩΟΙΟ

18. *Icon of the Virgin and Child, 'The Kardiotissa': a work of the Cretan painter Angelos. 15th c. Probably a copy of a Cretan miraculous icon.*

19. *St. Catherine. Cretan icon. 15th-16th century. The princess is represented with her attributes: the martyr's cross and wheel.*

20. *St. Anthony depicted standing full-length in an iconostasis door. This Cretan work of the 15th-16th century preserves the technique of the preceding period, as well as the nobility of, and reverence felt for, the ascetic figure.*

21. *Icon of the Hospitality of Abraham symbolizing the Holy Trinity. With its serene and lofty air, its concentrated geometric composition and stiff drapery, it represents a classical phase in Cretan painting of the first half of the 16th century.*

22. *Triptych of the Transfiguration flanked by the Tree of Jesse and the Vine. The simplicity of the shape and the lack of finish of the frame are much in keeping with the popular art character of 17th century painting in Central Greece.*

23. *The Virgin and the rescue at sea of Sior Ardavani. 17th century. Provenance: Ionian Islands. The icon, which represents both the Virgin in the role of protectress and the maritime incident, belongs to a type with a Western votive character.*

24. *Icon of the Virgin and Child, 'The Galaktotrophousa' by the monk Makarios of Galatista (1784). Typically Athonite work, in which the exactitude associated with a handicraftsman's work is particularly evident.*

25. *A didactic icon of popular art (1825). Its representation of the blind Eros and the Sirens shows how non-religious themes were still interpreted in the manner of mediaeval painting at the time of the Greek War of Independence. The work is by one Agapios Manganaris of Siphnos.*

22

23

24

25

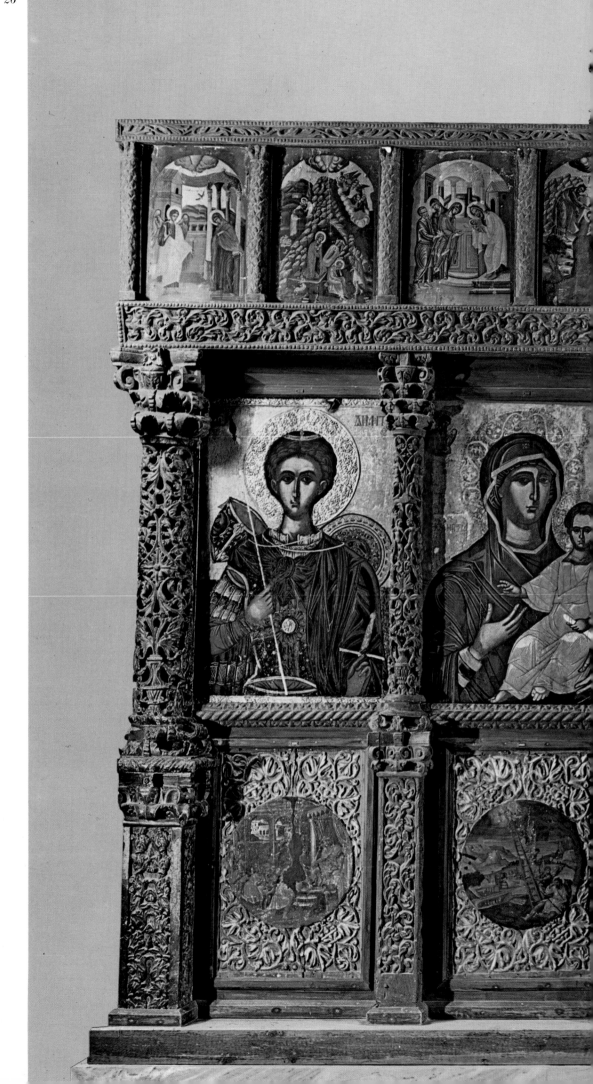

26. The wooden iconostasis, as developed in the 16th and 17th centuries, continued to be a well-constructed feature with lavish carving. The icons of Christ and the Virgin, dated 1680, are by the Cretan Emmanuel Tzanes. The Italicizing closure panels are by the Cretan artist, Elias Moskos, a contemporary of Tzanes, who worked in Zakynthos. Saint Demetrios, left, may be attributed to Frangos Katelanos (mid 16th century), while the Deesis, right, dates from the 15th century. The Dodecaorton (Cycle of the Twelve Feasts) is a Zakynthian work of the 17th century.

27. *Jewellery from a treasure found in Mytilene, dated by means of gold coins to the early 7th century. Roman traditions prevail in the necklaces, whereas the buckles have a clearly Byzantine character.*

28. *Silver plate with incised cross and ivy tendrils. Provenance: Mytilene treasure.*

29. *'Trulla'. 7th century vessel with non-Christian incised representations. Provenance: Mytilene treasure.*

28

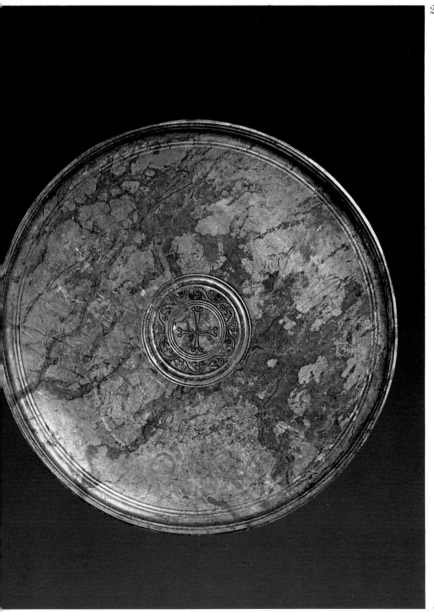

29

31

30. Gospel book cover from Trebizond with features associated with different periods. Three of the corner adornments, consisting of embossed medallions with arabesques, are of the 14th-15th century, the fourth (top right), which is less skillfully worked, of a later period. The central cross with the engraved representations is of the 16th-17th century. The correct position for the medallions would be Christ in the middle and the angel above, as appropriate in a Deesis representation.

31. Pastoral staff of Bishop Neophytos of Adrianople (1653-1658) decorated with precious stones, rubies and enamels. Work of fine quality. Provenance: possibly Constantinople. Painted enamels in the medallions: Christ, the Virgin, three hierarchs and St. John.

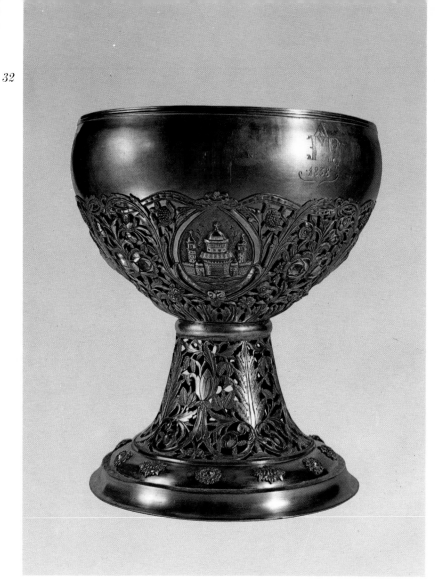

32. 19th century silver censer with lid and engraved and open-work decoration. Western influences are apparent. Provenance: Asia Minor relics.

33. Silver vessel for Holy Water from the Monastery of Prodromos, near Serrai. Date: 1838. Embossed representations of the monastery and other decoration in open-work.

34. 17th century spherical crown of chandelier from Kythera. Collection of the Christian Archaeological Society. Elegant incised decoration with foliate themes.

35. Large pyx (artophorion) from the Metropolis, Adrianople. The rough and unskilled silver and gilt relief contrasts with the Homeric style metrical inscription finely wrought in enamel which commemorates the donor, Neophytos, Bishop of Adrianople (1669).

36. Large cross, dated 1654, with fine enamel decoration which does not wholly match the unskilled wood-carved representations of the Feasts.

36

37

38

37. *The Entry into Jerusalem. Detail from a silver-thread embroidered stole depicting the Twelve Feasts. Although lacking variety in technique, it preserves an artistic accuracy and a serene and well-balanced composition which is nevertheless entirely flat in its simple chromatic range.*

38. *Gold-thread 'Aer' from Thessalonike. Outstanding work of art of the early 14th century. This liturgical piece of cloth was destined to cover the chalice with the bread and wine; consequently, the representations of the Holy Community and Christ-Amnos (The Lamb) refer to the mystery of the Eucharist. Later, this kind of cloth, with the same central representation, served as an epitaphios during Holy Week. The embroidery has been executed so skillfully that the subjects are rendered in the manner of a painting, while fully exploiting the possibilities of expression provided by the special technique, with its use of costly materials, gold and silver wire, silks, and a variety of stitches with different reflections which create an effect of delicate constantly changing tones.*

39. *Gospel book cover, dated 1755, with adjoining moulded little plaques framed with filigree and coloured stones. The Despotic Feasts and saints are represented. Their order must have been altered when the book cover was repaired at some later date.*